Ready to Learn

Story Problems

How To Play

1 Press the Power button to turn the SD-X Reader on or off. The LED will light up when the SD-X Reader is on.

2 Touch the volume buttons found on this page to adjust the volume.

3 Touch words and pictures on the page to hear audio. Touch this icon to start an activity:

4 After two minutes of inactivity, the SD-X Reader will beep and go to sleep.

5 If the batteries are low, the SD-X Reader will beep twice and the LED will start blinking. Replace the batteries by following the instructions on the next page. The SD-X Reader uses two AAA batteries.

6 To use headphones or earbuds, plug them into the headphone jack on the SD-X Reader.

Volume

Publications International, Ltd.

SD·X
INTERACTIVE

Battery Information
Includes two replaceable AAA batteries (UM-4 or LR03).

Battery Installation
1. Open battery door with small flat-head or Phillips screwdriver.
2. Install new batteries according to +/- polarity. If batteries are not installed properly, the device will not function.
3. Replace battery door; secure with small screw.

Battery Safety
Batteries must be replaced by adults only. Properly dispose of used batteries. See battery manufacturer for disposal recommendations. Do not dispose of batteries in fire; batteries may explode or leak. Do not mix alkaline, standard (carbon-zinc), or rechargeable (nickel-cadmium) batteries. Do not mix old and new batteries. Only recommended batteries of the same or equivalent type should be used. Remove weakened or dead batteries. Never short-circuit the supply terminals. Non-rechargeable batteries are not to be recharged. Do not use rechargeable batteries. If batteries are swallowed, in the USA, promptly see a doctor and have the doctor phone 1-202-625-3333 collect. In other countries, have the doctor call your local poison control center. This product uses 2 AAA batteries (2 X 1.5V = 3.0 V). Use batteries of the same or equivalent type as recommended. The supply terminals are not to be short-circuited. Batteries should be changed when sounds mix, distort, or become otherwise unintelligible as batteries weaken. The electrostatic discharge may interfere with the sound module. If this occurs, please simply restart the sound module by pressing any key.

In Europe, the dustbin symbol indicates that batteries, rechargeable batteries, button cells, battery packs, and similar materials must not be discarded in household waste. Batteries containing hazardous substances are harmful to the environment and to health. Please help to protect the environment from health risks by telling your children to dispose of batteries properly and by taking batteries to local collection points. Batteries handled in this manner are safely recycled.

Warning: Changes or modifications to this unit not expressly approved by the party responsible for compliance could void the user's authority to operate the equipment.

NOTE: This equipment has been tested and found to comply with the limits for a Class B digital device, pursuant to Part 15 of the FCC Rules. These limits are designed to provide reasonable protection against harmful interference in a residential installation. This equipment generates, uses, and can radiate radio frequency energy and, if not installed and used in accordance with the instructions, may cause harmful interference to radio communications. However, there is no guarantee that interference will not occur in a particular installation. If this equipment does cause harmful interference to radio or television reception, which can be determined by turning the equipment off and on, the user is encouraged to try to correct the interference by one or more of the following measures: Reorient or relocate the receiving antenna. Increase the separation between the equipment and receiver. Connect the equipment into an outlet on a circuit different from that to which the receiver is connected. Consult the dealer or an experienced radio TV technician for help.

Writer: Beth Goers

Cover illustrated by Olin Kidd

Illustrator: Olin Kidd

Louis Weber, C.E.O., Publications International, Ltd.
7373 North Cicero Avenue   Ground Floor, 59 Gloucester Place
Lincolnwood, Illinois 60712   London W1U 8JJ

Customer Service:
1-888-724-0144 or customer_service@pilbooks.com
www.pilbooks.com

SD-X Interactive is a registered trademark in the United States and Canada.

Manufactured in China.

8 7 6 5 4 3 2 1
ISBN-10: 1-4508-4683-1
ISBN-13: 978-1-4508-4683-7

PLAY

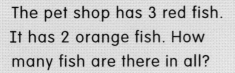

The pet shop has 3 red fish. It has 2 orange fish. How many fish are there in all?

```
  3  red fish
+ 2  orange fish
─────
  5  fish in all
```

```
  6  purple fish
- 4  purple fish
─────
  2  fish are left
```

The pet shop had 6 purple fish. It sold 4 purple fish. How many purple fish are left?

Monkey buys 2 fish. Giraffe buys 1 fish. Touch the number that tells how many fish they buy in all.

```
  2  fish
+ 1  fish
─────
```

2 3 4

Addition Story Problems

Elephant buys 6 green apples and 3 red apples. How many apples does Elephant buy in all?

6 apples
+3 apples
___
9 apples in all

5 bananas
+3 bananas
___
8 bananas in all

Monkey buys two bunches of bananas. One bunch has 5 bananas. The other bunch has 3 bananas. How many bananas does Monkey have in all?

Lizard sees 2 jars of honey on a shelf. She sees 2 more jars on another shelf. How many jars does Lizard see in all?

2 jars
+2 jars
_____
☐ jars
in all

The store has 4 large windows and 3 small windows. How many windows are there in all?

4 windows
+3 windows
_____
☐ windows
in all

Owl buys 1 orange at the store today. He bought 2 oranges yesterday. How many oranges does Owl buy in all?

1 orange
+2 oranges
_____
☐ oranges
in all

1 2 3 4 5 6 7 8 9 10

Subtraction Story Problems

PLAY

Five birds sit on a branch. Three birds fly away. How many birds are left on the branch?

5 birds
-3 birds
_____
2 birds
are left

7 dogs
-4 dogs
_____
3 dogs
are left

Seven dogs go to the ice cream shop. Four dogs go inside. How many dogs are left?

Lizard has 9 gumballs. She gives 6 gumballs away. How many gumballs are left?

9 gumballs
-6 gumballs
_____
2 3 4 gumballs
are left

Giraffe buys an ice cream cone with 3 scoops. She eats 2 scoops. How many scoops of ice cream are left?

3 scoops
-2 scoops
_____

1 **2** **3**

scoop is left

Monkey has 4 cherries on his banana split. He eats 2 cherries. How many cherries are left?

4 cherries
-2 cherries
_____

4 **3** **2**

cherries are left

Elephant has an ice cream cone with 6 scoops. He drops 1 scoop. How many scoops are left?

6 scoops
-1 scoop
_____

4 **5** **6**

scoops are left

Plus and Minus Clues

PLAY

Addition clue words:

in all   **all together**

Subtraction clue words:

are left   **more**   **less**

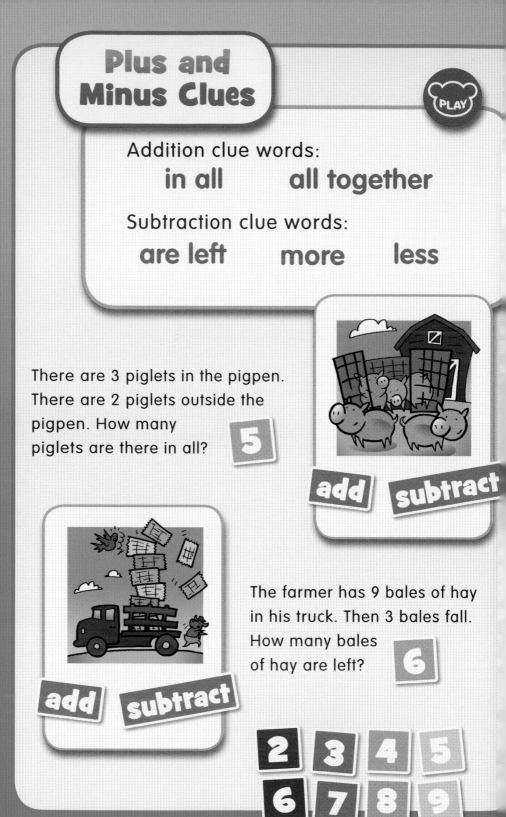

There are 3 piglets in the pigpen. There are 2 piglets outside the pigpen. How many piglets are there in all?

5

add   **subtract**

The farmer has 9 bales of hay in his truck. Then 3 bales fall. How many bales of hay are left?

6

add   **subtract**

2 **3** **4** **5**
6 **7** **8** **9**

There are 6 cows in the barn on the farm. There are 2 horses. How many animals are there in all?

?

add subtract

add subtract

Each cow needs 10 bales of hay a week. Each horse needs 12 bales of hay. How many more bales does a horse need?

?

One hen lays 5 eggs. Another hen lays 4 eggs. How many eggs do they have all together?

?

add

subtract

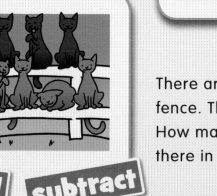

add subtract

There are 3 black cats on the fence. There are 4 orange cats. How many cats are there in all?

?

Fill in the Blank

Use **addition** or **subtraction** to find the missing words.

PLAY

| |
| one |
| two |
| three |
| four |
| five |
| six |
| seven |
| eight |
| nine |
| ten |

There are six red marbles and three yellow marbles in a jar. The jar has ___ marbles in all.

Monkey had eight purple marbles. He gave ___ to Giraffe. Monkey has five purple marbles left.

Owl has ___ blue marbles. Elephant has two blue marbles. They have four blue marbles all together.

Lizard has four red marbles. She has three green marbles. Lizard has ___ marbles in all.

Giraffe had nine yellow marbles. She gave Ostrich four marbles. Giraffe has ___ yellow marbles left.

Touch the True Sentence

PLAY

Monkey brought 2 cups of sugar. Elephant brought 5 cups of sugar. How many cups do they have in all?

3+5=7   2+5=7

There were 12 eggs in the carton. The recipe used 6 eggs. How many eggs are left over?

12−6=6   12+6=10

Lizard made a batch of 14 cookies. Owl made 6 cookies. How many more cookies did Lizard make?

14−6=8   13−6=8

There are 4 dirty spoons in the sink. Giraffe adds 2 more. How many dirty spoons are there all together?

4+2=7   4+2=6

Giraffe needs 5 cups of milk to make a cake. She only has 3 cups of milk. How many more cups of milk does Giraffe need to make her cake?

5−3=2   5+2=3

Favorite Fruits

Miss Moose makes a graph. She asks her students to pick a favorite fruit. Elephant picks apples as his favorite fruit. Giraffe and Owl pick oranges. Lizard picks strawberries as her favorite fruit. Monkey and Ostrich choose bananas. Three more students pick apples and one more student picks oranges as favorite fruits. Use this information to answer the questions.

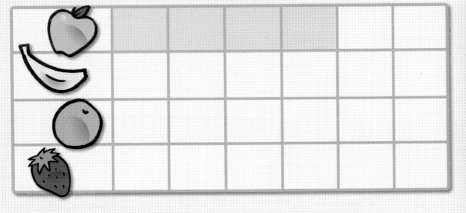

Each shaded box represents a student who picks apples. There are 4 students that pick apples.

 How many students pick bananas as their favorite?  2 3 4

 How many students pick oranges?  5 4 3

 How many students pick strawberries?  1 2 3

Do more students like apples or bananas?

apples   bananas

Which fruit does the class like the least?

apples   bananas
oranges   strawberries

Which fruit does the class like the most?

apples   bananas
oranges   strawberries

How many more students choose oranges than strawberries?

1   2   3

How many students does Miss Moose collect data from in all?

8   9   10

Monkey sees 3 dogs at the game. He sees 6 more dogs on the way home. How many dogs does Monkey see in all?

$$3+7=11$$ **TRUE** **FALSE**

The game lasts 40 minutes. The team plays for 20 minutes. How many more minutes are left in the game?

$$40-20=20$$ **TRUE** **FALSE**

The Pineapples team has 4 timeouts to use in the game. They used 1 timeout in the first half. How many timeouts does the team have left?

$$4-1=2$$ **TRUE** **FALSE**

The Pineapples score 4 points in the first half. They score 3 points in the second half. How many points do they score in all?

$$4+3=7$$ **TRUE** **FALSE**

How many more points did the Pineapples score in the first half than in the second half?

$$4-3=2$$ **TRUE** **FALSE**

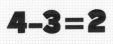

Missing Numbers

There are ten players on the team. Five players leave the field to sit on the bench. How many players are left on the field?

$$10-5=?$$

4 **5** **6**

Giraffe brought 6 juice boxes. She and Ostrich have 9 juice boxes all together. How many juice boxes did Ostrich have?

$$6+?=9$$

1 **2** **3**

Owl brought 8 sticks of gum to the game. He gave 2 sticks away. How many sticks does Owl have left?

$$8-2=?$$

6 **4** **7**

Elephant has some apples. Lizard has 7 apples. Elephant and Lizard have 9 apples in all. How many apples does Elephant have?

$$?+7=9$$

2 **3** **5**

PLAY

2-Digit Addition Story Problems

Monkey drove 32 miles to Bear City. Then he drove another 11 miles. How many miles did Monkey drive in all?

Add the ones first.

$$\begin{array}{r} 32 \\ +11 \\ \hline 3 \end{array}$$

Then add the tens.

$$\begin{array}{r} 32 \\ +11 \\ \hline 43 \end{array}$$

PLAY

There are 12 houses on one side of the street. There are 6 houses on the other side. How many houses are there in all?

$$\begin{array}{r} 12 \\ +6 \\ \hline \end{array}$$

18 **19** **20**

$$\begin{array}{r} 21 \\ +8 \\ \hline \end{array}$$

28 **29** **30**

Elephant drives 21 miles in the morning. He drives 8 miles in the afternoon. How many miles does Elephant drive in all?

Monkey sees 16 animals on his way to Bear City. He sees 41 animals on the way back. How many animals does Monkey see all together?

$$\begin{array}{r} 16 \\ +41 \\ \hline \end{array}$$

52 **55** **57**

2-Digit Subtraction Story Problems

Monkey is taking an elevator going up to the 25th floor. The elevator stops on the 14th floor. How many floors are left?

Subtract the ones first.

$$\begin{array}{r} 25 \\ -14 \\ \hline 1 \end{array}$$

Then subtract the tens.

$$\begin{array}{r} 25 \\ -14 \\ \hline 11 \end{array}$$

PLAY

Monkey is taking the stairs to see his friend who lives on the 28th floor. He stops on the 10th floor to take a break. How many more flights of stairs does Monkey need to climb to reach his friend?

$$\begin{array}{r} 28 \\ -10 \\ \hline ? \end{array}$$

$$\begin{array}{r} 29 \\ -7 \\ \hline ? \end{array}$$

Giraffe is taking an elevator from the bottom floor up to the 29th floor. The elevator stops on the 7th floor to let some passengers out. How many more floors must Giraffe go to reach the 29th floor?

Owl is flying up to the 23rd floor. He stops on the 13th floor to rest his wings. How many more floors will Owl fly up to get to the 23rd floor?

$$\begin{array}{r} 23 \\ -13 \\ \hline ? \end{array}$$

10   18   22

Greater Than

PLAY

Monkey rode his bike 4 miles on Saturday. He rode 5 miles on Sunday. Lizard rode her bike 3 miles on Saturday. She rode 8 miles on Sunday.

How many miles did Monkey ride in all?

7 **8** **9**

How many miles did Lizard ride in all?

10 **11** **12**

Who rode a greater number of miles in all?

Monkey **Lizard**

Elephant rode his bike 5 miles on Monday. He rode 8 miles on Tuesday. Giraffe rode 3 miles on Monday. She rode 4 miles on Tuesday.

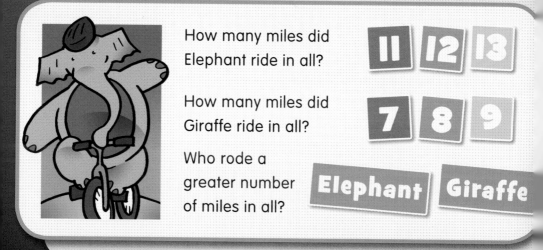

How many miles did Elephant ride in all?

11 **12** **13**

How many miles did Giraffe ride in all?

7 **8** **9**

Who rode a greater number of miles in all?

Elephant **Giraffe**

Less Than

Ostrich rode 8 miles on Wednesday and 2 miles on Thursday. Owl rode 4 miles on Wednesday and 7 miles on Thursday.

How many miles did Ostrich ride in all?

9 **10** **11**

How many miles did Owl ride in all?

11 **12** **13**

Who rode a lesser number of miles in all?

Ostrich **Owl**

Giraffe rode 12 miles in the morning. In the afternoon, she rode 11 miles. Monkey rode 16 miles in the morning. He rode 13 miles in the afternoon.

How many miles did Giraffe ride in all?

22 **23** **24**

How many miles did Monkey ride in all?

29 **30** **31**

Who rode a lesser number of miles in all?

Giraffe **Monkey**

Adding Fractions

PLAY

Giraffe has a pizza cut into 3 equal slices. She eats 1 slice and gives 1 slice to Ostrich to eat. What fraction of the pizza is eaten?

Lizard has a pizza cut into 2 equal slices. She eats 1 slice. What fraction of the pizza does Lizard eat?

Monkey and Elephant get a pizza cut into 4 equal slices. Monkey eats 1 slice. Elephant eats 2 slices. What fraction of the pizza do they eat all together?

Ostrich gets a pizza cut into 3 equal slices. Ostrich eats 1 piece and is taking the rest home to eat tomorrow. What fraction of the pizza does Ostrich eat today?

$$\frac{3}{4} \quad \frac{1}{2} \quad \frac{1}{3} \quad \frac{2}{3}$$

Subtracting Fractions

PLAY

Elephant has a pie cut into fourths. He eats 1 piece and gives 2 pieces away. What fraction of the pie is left?

$\frac{1}{3}$ $\frac{3}{4}$ $\frac{1}{4}$

$\frac{2}{3}$ $\frac{1}{2}$ $\frac{1}{3}$

Owl has a pie cut into halves. He eats 1 piece. What fraction of the pie is left?

Lizard has a pie cut into thirds. She eats 1 piece. What fraction of the pie is left?

$\frac{2}{3}$ $\frac{1}{4}$ $\frac{1}{3}$

$\frac{1}{3}$ $\frac{1}{4}$ $\frac{3}{4}$

Monkey has a pie cut into fourths. He eats 1 piece. What fraction of the pie is left?

Adding Money

PLAY

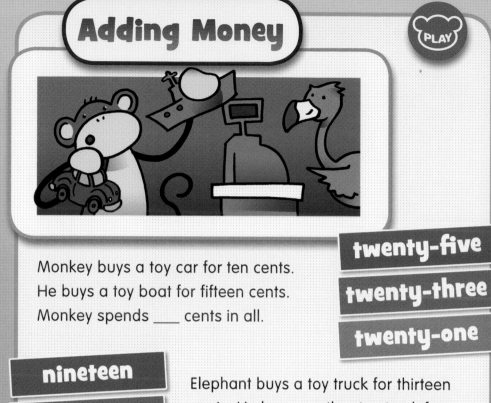

Monkey buys a toy car for ten cents.
He buys a toy boat for fifteen cents.
Monkey spends ____ cents in all.

twenty-five

twenty-three

twenty-one

nineteen

twenty-nine

thirty-nine

Elephant buys a toy truck for thirteen
cents. He buys another toy truck for
sixteen cents. Elephant spends ____
cents in all on toy trucks.

Giraffe buys a toy ball and a toy whistle.
The ball costs twenty-five cents and the
whistle costs twelve cents. Both toys
cost ____ cents all together.

twenty-seven

thirty-six

thirty-seven

seventy-two

seventy-three

sixty-three

Owl buys a toy bear for fifty cents.
He buys a toy plane for twenty-three
cents. Owl spends
____ cents in all.

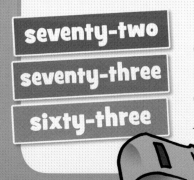

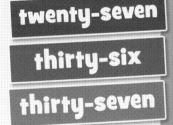

Subtracting Money

PLAY

Monkey had 99¢. He spent 25¢ on candy. How much does Monkey have left?

Owl had 55¢ when he went into the store. He spent 25¢ on a cookie. How many cents did Owl have when he left the store?

Lizard had 89¢. She bought a lollipop for 13¢. How many cents does Lizard have now?

Elephant had 66¢. He bought a cupcake for 30¢. How many cents does Elephant have left?

Giraffe had 40¢. She bought two candy canes for 10¢ each. How many cents does Giraffe have left over?

20¢

30¢

36¢

74¢

76¢

There are 10 red vans in the parking lot. There are 7 blue vans. How many vans are there in all?

16 17 18

Giraffe saw 15 white cars in the parking lot. Then 5 white cars drove away. How many white cars are left?

10 11 12

Rhino sold 20 tickets for his parking lot on Monday. He sold 17 tickets on Tuesday. Lizard sold 16 tickets for her parking lot on Monday and 23 on Tuesday.

How many tickets did Rhino sell in all?

27 30 37

How many tickets did Lizard sell in all?

39 40 49

Who sold a greater number of tickets total?

Rhino Lizard

Monkey has 88¢. He spends 20¢ on a ticket for the parking lot. How many cents does Monkey have left?

58¢ 60¢ 68¢